AMERICAN
COASTLINES

WILLIAM K SMITHEY

GALLERY BOOKS
An Imprint of W. H. Smith Publishers Inc.
112 Madison Avenue
New York City 10016

Text
William K. Smithey

Editorial
Gill Waugh

Design
Clive Dorman

Production
Ruth Arthur
David Proffit
Sally Connolly
Andrew Whitelaw

Jacket Design
Claire Leighton

Commissioning Editor
Andrew Preston

Director of Production
Gerald Hughes

Publishing Assistant
Edward Doling

Director of Publishing
David Gibbon

Photography
Planet Earth Pictures:
J. Brian Alker 4, 19 *bottom*; Kurt Amsler 26 *left*; Robert Arnold 11.
bottom; Pete Atkinson back cover; Mark Conlin 15 *top*, 25; D. Robert
Franz 16; Al Giddings 29 *top*; Daniel W. Gorshall 17 *top*; Anthony
Joyce 23 *top*; Robert A. Juriet 7 *bottom*; A. Kerstitch 26 *right*, 30 *top*;
James M. King 31 *right*; John Lythgoe 22 *top*; Ken Lucas 12, 14, 21;
David Jesse McChesney 6-7 *top*, 31 *left*, 32; Krov Menuhin 29 *bottom*;
Doug Perrine 18 *left*; Linda Pitkin 27; David A. Ponton 22 *bottom*;
Keith Scholey 18 *right*; William K. Smithey 10,13, 17 *bottom*; P. V.
Tearle 11 *top*; Gilbert van Ryckevorsel 15 *bottom*; James Watt 8, 30
bottom; Dorian Weisel 5; Rodney Wood 28; Joyce Wilson 9, 19 *top*, 23
bottom pictures; Norbert Wu 6, 24.

CLB 2485
This edition published in 1990 by Gallery Books,
an imprint of WH Smith Publishers, Inc,
112 Madison Avenue, New York 10016.
© 1990 Colour Library Books Ltd, Godalming, Surrey, England.
All rights reserved.
Colour separations by Scantrans Pte Ltd, Singapore.
Printed and bound by New Interlitho, Italy.
ISBN 0 8317 6977 7

Gallery Books are available for bulk purchase for sales promotions
and premium use. For details write or telephone
the Manager of Special Sales, WH Smith Publishers, Inc,
112 Madison Avenue, New York, New York 10016 (212) 532-6600.

CONTENTS

INTRODUCTION 5

THE COASTAL FOOD CHAIN 10

COASTAL WILDLIFE HABITATS 12

PROTECTED WATERS 20

PACIFIC KELP FOREST 24

CORAL REEFS 26

MARINE MAMMALS 28

INTRODUCTION

Seventy percent of the earth's surface is covered by water. At the margin of the land, where the earth and sea meet, there is constant change. Waves and tides, rocks and sand, fresh and salt water all combine in this dynamic setting. The coastline may be exposed to constant pounding of waves or protected from them, rise abruptly as cliffs or emerge gently as a wide sandy beach. It is clear that no two places along this vast margin are the same.

Throughout geologic time, the contours of a shoreline are constantly refashioned. Sea levels fall or rise as more or less water is held in glaciers and the polar ice caps. Rivers, past and present, also play a role as they deliver countless tons of silt and sand, which are dumped as they reach the sea. Occasional hurricanes can remake large areas, wiping out barrier islands as they pass. Earthquakes can raise or lower the shoreline in an instant.

Less dramatic change is evident as well. Tides rise and fall with regularity. Endless waves, each different from the last, end long journeys by breaking on the shore. The wind sculpts sand dunes, slowly burying plants and obliterating any sign of man.

In total, the Pacific, Atlantic and Gulf coasts of the United States constitute a staggering number of miles of shoreline, with plants and animals living along nearly all of it. From marine mammals to tiny invertebrates, from fish to shellfish, the interface between land and ocean is uncommonly rich in plant and animal life.

Facing page: the sandy beach at Jupiter Island, Florida. The coastline of Hawaii (below) is constantly changing as molten lava flows into the sea.

PACIFIC COAST

The Pacific coast of North America consists of 56,000 miles of shoreline (4,000 miles in a direct line), stretching from the glacial fjords of Alaska to the sandy beaches of Southern California.

Because glaciers were once found at sea level as far south as Puget Sound, in Washington State, this region serves as a convenient boundary. North of Puget Sound the coastline comprises rugged fjords, coastal islands and channels; sandy beaches and mud flats are rare. South of Puget Sound the coast is exposed to the battering of Pacific storms and alternates between rocky headlands and a few large river estuaries. Sand dunes are found along the entire west coast, but are best developed along the coast of Oregon and southern Washington. Further to the south the coast becomes more or less straight and is punctuated by Humboldt, San Francisco and Monterey bays. Finally, the sandy beaches of the southern California coast are bordered mostly by low sea cliffs.

Right: abrupt cliffs, sculpted by the constant motion of the waves and tides of a restless sea. Below: the sun setting off the Pacific coast, California.

6

ATLANTIC COAST

Ancient glaciers have rendered Cape Cod, like Puget Sound, something of a demarcation. To the north, rocky shores predominate while to the south, outcroppings of rock continue as far as Rhode Island but diminish until no natural rocky shoreline exists south of the Middle Atlantic States. Sandy beaches are rare to the north.

From New Jersey to northern Florida, salt marshes are common in protected waters behind barrier islands and in bays and estuaries. A large portion of the Atlantic coast is bordered by sandy beaches. From Labrador to Mexico estuaries abound and bays indent the shoreline.

Coral reefs, which are formed by living organisms, occur only in warm water off southern Florida and the Florida Keys. Because of these reefs, the sand of southern beaches is composed of materials different from those that form the more northerly ones. This material is mostly calcite, or calcium carbonate, which makes up the skeletons of the animals that form the reef.

Below: sea stacks, island remnants of a former coastline, rise from the foggy Pacific in Olympic National Park, Washington.

GULF OF MEXICO COAST

The Gulf of Mexico is almost an inland sea, with Florida, Cuba and the Yucatan Peninsula of Mexico nearly pinching it off from the Atlantic Ocean. The Florida coast of the Gulf is mostly of living origin; the rest of the Gulf Coast is composed of sandy and muddy sediments derived from ancient rivers and glaciers. Along the Louisiana, Texas and northern Mexican coasts ten major rivers carry huge sediment loads into the Gulf. These deposits, which include the Mississippi delta, make the Gulf fundamentally different from the other two coasts. Barrier islands border much of the Gulf and create obstacles for storm waves. The Gulf is known for its hurricanes, which frequently wash over low islands causing great destruction to wildlife, vegetation and human development.

The coast of the Gulf of Mexico (right) is rich in history. Amerigo Vespucci, who lent his name to the continent, was apparently the first European to actually visit this unique shoreline. Long before the Spanish first explored the coastline, however, the Aztecs had sailed the Gulf. The Gulf shoreline varies greatly in its topography, vegetation, geology and marine life, including barrier islands and sandy beaches as well as coral beaches and salt marshes, and supports a rich assortment of marine animals and plants. The Gulf of Mexico was once home to five species of the great sea turtle (below). Hunted excessively by man, some of these species are now uncommon and the rest extinct.

THE COASTAL FOOD CHAIN

The basis of the ocean ecosystem, like that of the land, is the energy derived from sunlight. But unlike the familiar plants of the terrestrial ecosystem, the basic food of much of the ocean consists of microscopic, one-celled plants called phytoplankton. Because the quantity of light decreases substantially with depth, these plants, which serve as the "ocean's grass," are restricted to a fairly narrow zone near the surface.

Tiny animals called zooplankton feed on the phytoplankton. Some zooplankton are adult creatures that spend their entire lives swimming in the ocean as part of the zooplankton; others are larvae, the developmental stages of larger animals. After spending the early stages of life swimming near the surface, many of the surviving larvae will settle to the ocean floor to become bottom dwelling invertebrates. Thus the planktonic portion of these animals' lives serves to spread them over a wide area. The larvae of fish also spend time as zooplankton, eventually developing into adults.

Taken together these plankton fuel the ocean. Many marine invertebrates, a large and diverse collection of animals associated by their lack of a backbone, feed directly on plankton by passing sea water through delicate filters. Other predators, in turn, feed on the direct plankton consumers. Blue whales, the largest animals on earth, are carnivores that feed on krill, a form of zooplankton found in Antarctic waters.

Along the coastline, where the sunlight penetrates to the bottom, larger algae grow. These seaweeds provide important food and habitat for many coastal creatures. Most flowering plants live on the land but some, like surf grass, eel grass and cordgrass, are adapted to life in salty water.

Below: the sea palm, a marine algae. Krill (facing page top) thrive in the Arctic and Antarctic oceans, providing a source of food for larger animals. Facing page bottom: minute plankton form the base of the oceanic food chain.

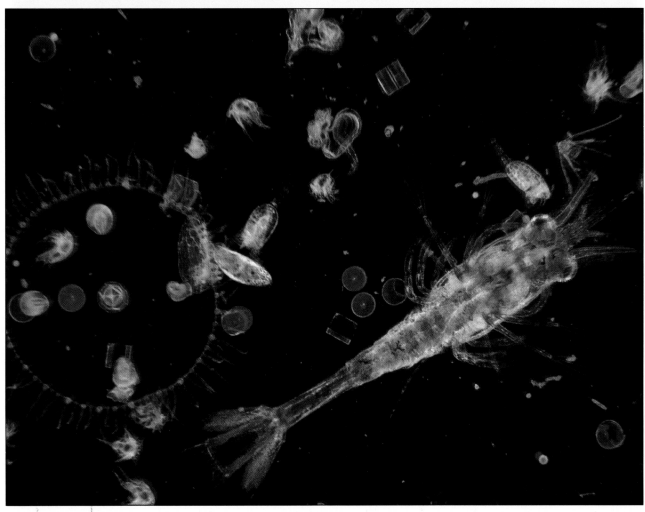

Coastal Wildlife Habitats

Rocky Coastlines

Much of the rocky coastline of both the Pacific and Atlantic oceans is subjected to the full fury of winter storms. Because the waves bring in an unending supply of food, this turbulent, rocky environment is the preferred habitat of many marine creatures. Real estate is so valuable along a rocky shore that the primary competition among attached organisms is for space, not, as in many other places in the natural world, for food.

Where tall cliffs tower above the water, sea birds converge, often in incredible numbers, to use the cliff face ledges as sites on which to breed and hatch their young. Colorful Atlantic and tufted puffins are found nesting in crevices near the tops of the cliffs. Thick-billed and common murres nest on thin cliff ledges and use their wings to "fly" underwater after prey. Least and whiskered auklets nest among the rock rubble at the cliff base. In turn, least auklets are important prey for peregrine falcons and glaucous-winged gulls.

A band of lichens and blue-green algae often marks the meeting of land and sea. Below this "black zone" lies the area usually affected by the extremes of high and low tides. Termed the intertidal zone, it is divided into three parts.

The uppermost part is an area that is usually dry but becomes inundated during the highest tides. It is not as well populated as the lower zones, but the periwinkle, a snail which feeds on blue-green algae, is common here. Another snail, the black tegula, is also found here feeding on fleshy algae. In turn, the black limpet attaches itself to the black tegula and feeds on the microscopic algae that grow on tegula shells. Because this area is seldom affected by ocean water, land-based insects can be found feeding in this area.

Barnacles often mark the transition from the upper to the middle intertidal area, where they live firmly attached to rocks. They subsist by filtering food using specially adapted legs. Barnacles are exceptional examples of adaptation to the intertidal environment and can extend all the way up to the splash zone, an area that seawater seldom reaches and, therefore, where feeding opportunities are extremely limited. Limpets, which are marine snails with cone-shaped shells, move among the barnacles, browsing on algae.

Below: California sea lions gathering on the rocky coast of the Farallon Islands off San Francisco. Thick-billed murres (facing page) lay eggs and raise their young on precipitous cliffs above the Bering Sea on Saint Paul Island, Alaska.

Below the barnacles, mussels become the predominate filter feeders. Mussels anchor themselves against the surf using bundles of sticky threads that are attached to the rock as well as to surrounding mussels. The tangle of mussels and threads forms a mat in which sediment accumulates and small animals, such as worms and minute crustaceans, live. Sea palms, marine algae that resemble miniature palm trees, survive the pounding of waves by anchoring themselves firmly among the mussels.

In this middle area along the Pacific coast the striped shore crab of southern California and the purple shore crab of the Pacific Northwest are common. Hermit crabs, which live in snail shells, are residents of tide pools in this area.

While the high tide line dictates the upper limit of mussel patches, the lower limit is set by sea stars, which prey upon them. Sea stars use their five arms to steadily pull apart the two halves of the mussel's shell. Once the shells are parted, the sea star pushes its bag-like stomach, inside out, into the mussel to slowly dissolve and then eat the contents. Because sea stars cannot feed out of water, mussels only begin to dominate several feet

above the low tide mark.

Sea cucumbers and their spiny relatives the urchins are commonly found in the final intertidal area, the lower intertidal zone. This zone is occasionally exposed to the air but only briefly, during the lowest tides. Sea stars are also common in this area.

Some birds are adapted to feeding on the inhabitants of the intertidal zone. The American oystercatcher feeds by inserting its bill between the two shells of mussels. Ruddy turnstones feed in the rocky intertidal by flipping over stones and eating the worms, mollusks, snails and crustaceans found underneath.

Beyond the lower intertidal zone lies the submerged subtidal zone. In the Pacific, several species of a giant limpet called abalone can be found attached to rocks. Abalone, which grow to be several inches long, are edible, and exploitation by man has severely reduced their numbers. The formidable northern lobster is found in the North Atlantic subtidal. Weighing as much as forty-five pounds, it has two dissimilar pincers; one for cracking hard prey and a sharper one used to rip prey or plant material apart.

Facing page top: goose barnacles with filter-feeding legs extended. Hermit crabs (facing page bottom) occupy empty shells. Above: brightly colored sea cucumbers, found in the lower intertidal zone. The pincers of the northern lobster (below) are dissimilar and serve different purposes.

SANDY BEACHES

Of all the seaside habitats, the sandy beach changes the most and the most rapidly. While we often think of beaches as being made strictly of sand, they can also consist of shells, or shell fragments, cobblestones, mud, coral or a mixture of these components.

Waves wash constantly over the intertidal area of a sandy beach, keeping it in perpetual motion. Life in the wash zone is left to specialized animals such as the mole crab, whose flattened shape is perfectly adapted for life among sand grains. Specialized worms, which feed by eating the sand and digesting the thin organic film that grows on it, and crustaceans also make the sandy intertidal their home. The edible pismo clam is found in sand flats from central California south to Baja California.

Countless shorebirds feed along a sandy beach.

Birds such as curlews, godwits and sandpipers all have bills of different lengths and this helps to limit direct competition between them as they probe for creatures beneath the sand. Feeding behavior, too, helps to avoid rivalry. The curved bill of an American avocet is used to stir the bottom, snapping up small crustaceans, while plovers race behind the waves, picking as they go.

Birds, such as terns and gulls, fish just off a sandy beach. Pelicans dive into the water, trapping fish in their large bills, then tilt their bill down, allowing the salt water to drain out before they swallow the fish. Black skimmers fish by flying low, dragging the lower portion of their bill through the water.

The American avocet (below) feeds by sweeping its bill from side to side in the water. Brown pelicans (facing page top) nest on cliffs and fish in nearby waters. Facing page bottom: a black skimmer fishing in calm water.

Sandy Beach Visitors

Each spring millions of horseshoe crabs crawl ashore to spawn, arriving in the greatest numbers along quiet Atlantic beaches between Long Island and Virginia. During a high tide each female lays her eggs in a hole dug above the low tide line, while the male fertilizes them. Great flocks of birds such as sandpipers, sanderlings, red knots, and ruddy turnstones feed on the eggs. These shorebirds have evolved migration patterns that coincide with the annual spring arrival of the horseshoe crabs.

The loggerhead turtle, which ranges widely throughout the warm waters of the Atlantic and Pacific oceans, has evolved migratory patterns that allow it to feed on the spring concentration of adult horseshoe crabs. Historically, major nesting concentrations of loggerheads ranged along the Atlantic coast as far north as Virginia, but now they are limited to south of the Carolinas.

Birds, such as the least tern, nest along the sandy shore. The tern lays its eggs in a spot hollowed out among the sparse vegetation along sandy beaches. Its numbers have been reduced along the California coast south of San Francisco, where it has suffered from the ever-increasing presence of man.

At night, from March to August, on the second, third and fourth nights after each full and each new moon, California grunion come ashore to lay their eggs. After riding in on a wave, the female wriggles most of her body down into the wet sand, while the male curves himself around the exposed portion of her body and spawns. Since the grunion lays its eggs as the tides are diminishing, the eggs will not be touched by water until the next series of high tides. The eggs remain buried until they are agitated by wave action during the next high tides, nine or ten days later, at which point the larval fish emerge from the eggs and swim out to sea.

Other animals, such as the familiar jellyfish, may end up on sandy beaches by accident. When discovered stranded on a beach, jellyfish usually resemble nothing more than a blob, for they are really animals of open-ocean waters, where they feed by catching prey in their dangling tentacles. The by-the-wind-sailor is a jellyfish relative with a bright blue, diagonal sail on its back. Using this sail the jellyfish can actually tack like a sail boat in the open ocean. They can be trapped by storms and wrecked in large numbers on the beach, where the gelatinous part of the animal decomposes leaving behind the blue sail.

Sand Dunes

Coastal sand dunes form in areas where strong onshore winds blow beach sand over adjoining low-lying land. Because of poor footing and because water passes through quickly, few plants grow on sand dunes. Those that do must be able to tolerate saltwater spray, wind and occasional burial by sand. American dune grass possesses an extensive root system that anchors it to the sand. This allows it to become established early in the dune's formation and to flourish in this unstable environment. Pioneer vegetation stabilizes a dune for a succession of plants, including yellow sand verbena, beach pea and beach morning glory.

Propelled by the same winds that formed them, dunes can progress inland, covering everything in their path. To stabilize dunes, European beach grass was introduced at the turn of the century. This grows vigorously, altering the dune ecosystem. Between Heceta Head and Coos Bay, Oregon, some of the most extensive dunes in the world are found, extending for over fifty miles along the coast and stretching up to two and one half miles inland. European beach grass has taken over these dunes and it may cover them completely within one hundred years, permanently altering the dune ecosystem.

Facing page: (left) a loggerhead turtle returns to the sea and (right) a stranded jellyfish is food for a shorebird. Above: a railroad vine in bloom. Dunes, which are often altered by introduced plants and the use of vehicles, may be restored. Below: a dune restoration project in Florida.

PROTECTED WATERS

ESTUARIES

Estuaries occur where sea water and fresh water meet and mix. They take a number of forms, including sloughs, lagoons, sounds and bays. Deltas, mud flats and salt marshes are also parts of estuaries. These are among the earth's most productive areas, providing a habitat for a great variety of life.

Estuaries are not just homes for worms; commercially important animals are found in them as well. In the Atlantic, soft-shell clams and, in the Pacific, the large geoduck are sought-after delicacies. Commercially valuable fish also spend the early part of their life cycle in estuaries or, as in the case of salmon and steelhead, swim through them on their way upstream to spawn.

The Chesapeake Bay is the largest and most productive estuary in the United States. Salt water from the Atlantic combines with the input of 150 rivers and tributaries to sustain 2,700 species of plants and animals. The bay is also the most heavily used; millions of people live near its shores and the ports of Baltimore and Hampton Roads rank among the busiest in the country.

The Chesapeake is far more than just a port. One half of the United States catch of the edible blue crab comes from this bay. Blue crabs spawn in the salty southern part of the bay, then migrate to the fresher areas to grow. Each fall, huge numbers of Canada geese, ducks and tundra swans come to visit.

MUD FLATS

As turbid rivers laden with sediment flow into the ocean, they deposit their load to form mud flats. The character of these mud flats changes with the tides. As the tide recedes, fresh water predominates; as the tide returns, salt water displaces it. Some areas may be left high and dry during these daily changes, being covered only when the river floods or the tide is especially high. The result is a difficult place; an area where creatures must be able to withstand great changes in conditions. Because food is delivered to the estuary from both the sea and, via the river, the land, animals that can live under these conditions often flourish in immense numbers.

Many of the animals that live in an estuary are infauna, animals that live within the mud. The innkeeper worm feeds by pumping water past a net, which it spins in the opening of its U-shaped burrow. Other animals, including the small arrow goby fish, a scale worm and two species of crabs, share the burrow, giving the innkeeper its name.

Rays, skates and sharks also call these protected waters home. Stingrays, which blend well as they rest on the bottom, can inflict a painful sting using a venomous spine located in their tail.

As the tide goes out, the residents of a mud flat face their greatest peril. Shorebirds such as the short-billed dowitcher, the willet and the western sandpiper actively probe for mollusks, crustaceans and marine worms on exposed mud flats.

SALT MARSHES

Coastal salt marshes are relatively rare along the Pacific coast, but are common in areas along the central and southern Atlantic coast where rivers transport enormous amounts of sediment. Salt marshes are formed through the interaction of tidal forces and plants called halophytes, terrestrial plants that are adapted to salty soils. The plants in a salt marsh slow the transport of sediment, causing it to settle around them. By holding waste as it passes through, they help to degrade organic pollution.

Because the surface of a salt marsh is soft and muddy, much of the life adapted to this habitat lives inconspicuously in burrows. Other wildlife, including beaver, muskrat, deer, river otters and raccoons, which visit or live in salt marshes, are more easily observed. Reptiles, such as the diamondback terrapin, are also found here. Birds, some secretive, such as the clapper rail, and others more easily observed, such as the northern harrier or the snowy egret, use the marsh both to feed and to shelter.

Pickleweed tolerates the most saline conditions, and will grow along saltwater canals (facing page top). The river otter (facing page bottom), with its streamlined body, webbed feet and rudder-like tail, is superbly adapted to aquatic life. It is also at home on land and can roam far from water.

MANGROVE SWAMPS

Beginning in central Florida, mangrove swamps replace salt marshes in shallow, muddy areas. The mangrove swamps of southwestern Florida are among the most extensive in the world. In addition to the problems involved in growing in salt water, mangrove trees must also contend with mud so dense that it deprives their roots of oxygen.

Within their dense tangle of growth and their muddy floor, mangrove swamps harbor much wildlife. Fiddler crabs are abundant residents of mangrove swamps, retreating to burrows when the tide is in. The mangrove mud crab lives among the foliage. Some animals, such as the flat tree oyster, grow in clumps on the roots. Snails are common, feeding on decaying mangrove leaves.

Above the water, in the relative safety of the mangrove trees, birds make their nests. High in the trees, tricolored herons and snowy egrets breed in large colonies and feed in the swamp below. Near the waterline, white ibis and green herons can be found. Birds such as the wood stork, the double-crested cormorant and the brown pelican are also common residents.

BAYS

While many bays are also estuaries, they are often simply protected portions of coastal waters cut off from the full effect of ocean waves by the land. Because they avoid the full effect of storm waves, they are much quieter places for marine organisms to live. Bays also provide a safe and convenient place for ships and serve as the focus of many cities.

COASTAL BARRIERS

The sandy beaches, islands and peninsulas along the Atlantic and Gulf coasts are among the most dynamic natural landscapes on earth. Composed of loose sand, they are only held together by vegetation and gravity. Generally one side of a coastal barrier faces the open ocean, and is thus exposed to the fury of a storm or hurricane, while the other side faces a shallow lagoon or marsh.

Beach grass and sea oats are among the few species that can survive in the sand immediately facing the ocean. Further back, away from storm waves, where the sand is made more stable by vegetation, shrubs and even forests can develop.

Barrier islands are important breeding grounds for birds such as gulls, terns, skimmers and wading birds. Their shallow backwaters serve as significant spawning and nursery sites for fish such as the sandbar shark.

Facing page top: mangroves with their knee roots exposed by low tide in the Everglades, where the great egret (facing page bottom) may be found. Above: the tourist mecca of Honolulu rising from the shores of Pearl Harbor. Impervious to sand abrasion and salt spray, the sea oat (below) is an important stabilizer of dunes along the Gulf Coast. Below right: beach sunflowers growing in shifting sand.

PACIFIC KELP FOREST

Forests of giant kelp can be found along the open coasts of the Pacific in shallow water between eighteen and ninety feet deep. From the anchoring, root-like holdfasts, continuing up the connecting stem, or stipe, to the waving fronds that form a canopy at the surface, the kelp forest is teaming with life.

At the edge of the sea in the temperate waters off California, the spectacular beds of giant kelp grow at an amazing rate. With a growth rate of up to eighteen inches per day, giant kelp are the fastest-growing plants known. They are commercially harvested for a variety of purposes and can yield up to six tons per acre each year.

Of the more than 150 species of fish found along the California coast, fifty are common in the kelp forest. Several species of rockfish feed among the holdfasts, preying on other fish or invertebrates. The giant sea bass, which reach weights in excess of 500 pounds, forage along the stipe and into the kelp canopy while other fish, such as topsmelt, use the kelp as refuge.

The root-like kelp holdfasts provide a habitat for many invertebrates, including brittle stars, octopi, worms and a wide variety of sponges. Bryozoans, tiny encrusting organisms, grow in colonies on the kelp fronds and dazzling, colorful nudibranchs can also be found among them.

Sea urchins eat kelp and, left without predators, can cause extensive damage to kelp beds. Sea otters, however, feed on urchins and, where populations are allowed to exist, they keep the urchins in check. Sea otters also feed on crabs, clams and abalone, putting them in direct competition with man for these edible shellfish. Once an endangered species because of their valuable pelts, sea otter populations have now increased and seem to be stable.

Sea otters (below) wrap themselves in kelp to maintain their position while resting. Kelp grows in giant underwater forests (facing page) on the floor of the Pacific Ocean.

CORAL REEFS

Coral reefs are composed of calcium carbonate or lime, a compound deposited by such marine organisms as stony corals, coralline algae, tube-building worms and others. Corals, whose colonies are the main contributors to the reef, are close cousins of sea anemones. They are basically tubular creatures with a crowning set of tentacles that surround the mouth. As individuals grow, a hard lime cup is deposited, and neighboring cups merge until the entire colony fuses together. The shape of the colony varies from boulder- to treelike, and may even, depending on the species, resemble a mushroom.

As a coral colony grows, only the animals on its outermost surface remain alive. Once an animal has completed building its protective home, it sends out filaments which sprout a new coral polyp. As the new polyp grows, it covers and eventually destroys the one beneath it. And so it continues, the dead mass of older coral providing support for future generations.

Such great expanses of sedentary life inevitably attract animals to feed. Some of these, such as the blue parrotfish, which grinds up mouthfuls of coral and then extracts the polyps, are quite destructive. Sea stars turn the polyps into a soup, by secreting into them a digestive fluid that leaves the structure of the reef intact.

Other animals use the reef, with its network of branches, as a place in which to hide or to make their home. Invertebrates such as sponges and sea squirts attach themselves to the reef and feed by pumping water through themselves, extracting from it both food and oxygen. Sedentary worms, including feather duster worms and star tube worms, trap plankton by using extended, feathery antennae. At night, orange or green fire worms crawl from their hiding places to hunt living coral or colonial sea anemones.

Some reef creatures have developed cooperative relationships with their neighbors. Fish accumulate parasites on their scales, fins, and even the insides of their mouths. Invertebrates such as the red and white banded coral shrimp establish "cleaning stations" where the parasites are removed. The fish, some of whom might normally be expected to eat the shrimp, respond to characteristic movements such as antennae waving and signal back to the shrimp that they are ready to be cleaned. The neon goby, a small, brightly striped fish, also operates a "cleaning station." Perched on coral heads, it waits to remove parasitic crustaceans from fish such as the Nassau grouper.

Below left: the colorful angelfish, a common resident of shallow coral reefs, and (below) a banded shrimp. Facing page: the intricate latticework of the purple sea fan, a coral found attached to reef rocks below the low tide line.

MARINE MAMMALS

Although many marine mammals make their home in the offshore waters, many can, with a little patience and luck, be viewed from either a seaside cliff or the shore of a bay.

MANATEE

These massive, torpedo-shaped aquatic mammals are found in shallow coastal waters, rivers, bays and mangrove swamps along the Gulf and Atlantic coasts of the southeastern United States. They are an endangered species, of which the largest remaining populations occur in the warm water off Florida.

Manatees are vegetarians, consuming sixty to one hundred pounds of vegetation each day, by using their split lips to harvest the vegetation adeptly from the bottom. Although not particularly social animals, they do congregate in warm water during the winter.

WHALES AND DOLPHINS

In late summer, as the northern oceans in which they feed grow colder, gray whales begin the longest migration of any mammal. They undertake the 13,000-mile round trip to mate and give birth in the warm shallow lagoons of Baja California.

Gray whales are bottom feeders, spending the summer months ploughing the bottom and filtering out larger crustaceans and worms. They use a special filtering structure, or baleen, for feeding. The gray whale was hunted by early American whalers and nearly made extinct. Saved by a ban on hunting, the gray whale population is now stable at more than 11,000 animals.

The killer whale, also known as the orca, is found along parts of the entire coast of America. They hunt cooperatively in a social unit called a pod and eat almost any animal in the sea, including squid, fish, sharks, seals, sea lions, sea birds and walrus. They will also eat other whales. With their large fins sticking above the water, adult males are unmistakable.

Bottlenose dolphins can be seen riding the bow waves of ships, or even surfing. They are most often seen close to the shore and may even enter rivers and estuaries. They are remarkably unafraid of man. Along with killer whales, bottlenose dolphins are popular attractions at marine theme parks.

Up to fifteen feet in length, the manatee (below) is sustained purely on aquatic vegetation. Facing page top: a breaching humpback whale. Facing page bottom: a pod of killer whales.

Seals and Sea Lions

After spending most of the year feeding at sea as far south as San Diego, California, hundreds of thousands of northern fur seals return each summer to Alaska's Pribilof Islands. Older males, or bulls, weighing up to 600 pounds, arrive first, establishing territories in May or early June. They may not return to the ocean for fifty days, living off stored fat, and forsaking food and water to defend these territories. Pregnant females begin to arrive in mid-June and, commonly, between twenty and sixty gather on each territory. The females give birth within forty-eight hours of their arrival and then mate again within a week.

Life on a fur seal rookery is noisy and violent. Territorial bulls vigorously defend their territories against neighbors on all sides. Pups, which weigh twelve pounds at birth, are easily crushed as the giant males race from border to border. As the pups grow older, they separate into groups in quieter parts of the rookery, out of harm's way. Unbred females are kept on the territories by force and are allowed to leave to feed only after mating.

Harbor seals range over the entire Pacific coast and north of the Carolinas along the Atlantic coast. They eat fish such as rockfish, herring, flounders and salmon, following fish runs far upriver. When not hunting, they spend much of their time resting on beaches and rocky shores in groups of between a few and several hundred animals.

California sea lions are the trained seals of zoos and theme parks. They exhibit similar behavior in the wild, throwing objects and catching them on their noses. They are the fastest-moving of the marine carnivores.

Northern elephant seals were nearly exterminated for their oil by whalers. From one remaining colony comprising as few as fifty animals, they have recovered to reach a population of about 65,000. They are huge animals and, because of their size, can only crawl onto land along sandy beaches. Although they prefer offshore islands, their increased numbers have forced them onto mainland beaches.

Facing page top: California sea lions basking on coastal rocks. The harbor seal (facing page bottom) may dive to depths of 300 feet in search of food. Below: a young, non-territorial northern fur seal. Below right: a male northern elephant seal. Overleaf: a cormorant on Santa Cruz Island.